Saying Good-bye, Saying Hello...

When Your Family Is Moving

Written by
Michaelene Mundy

Illustrated by
R. W. Alley

ONE
CARING
PLACE

Abbey Press
St. Meinrad, IN 47577

*To Emmy, as she heads
from Indiana to New York*

Text © 2005 Michaelene Mundy
Illustrations © 2005 St. Meinrad Archabbey
Published by One Caring Place
Abbey Press
St. Meinrad, Indiana 47577

Library of Congress Catalog Number
2004117890

ISBN 0-87029-393-1

Printed in the United States of America

A Message to Parents, Teachers, and Other Caring Adults

We all have moved sometime in our lives, and we remember some of the feelings we had. In moving with children, we are there to help them feel safe and secure among all the hustle and bustle and the many changes ahead.

Depending on the child's age, it is best to tell him or her as soon as possible that a move is imminent, and why. You can help your child understand that things change, including where you live, but that the same people who love and care for them will continue to be a part of their lives.

As you pack up things, involve your children as much as possible. On move-in day, consider putting a child's room together first. The child can then busy himself or herself unpacking toys and books while you work on other areas. Also, it gives your child a retreat where he or she can be surrounded by familiar things, as the rest of the house may be in turmoil.

After your move, keeping as many routines as possible will help. You probably have a bed-time ritual that will continue wherever you are. At bedtime that first night, try to follow the usual routine—bath, snuggling in bed with your child while a story is read, talking about the day that has just ended, talking about the day that is to come and what you will be doing.

Of course, this may also be a hard time for you, the parents, even if the move will make your life better in the long run. Your children will pick up your reactions to the move quickly. As the adult, you can help the child recognize the fun and excitement of a move while recognizing the fears of new places and people and the sadness of good-byes. You can help your child say "good-bye" to the "old" neighborhood and "hello" to the new one. In the long run, you will find that in helping your children make a happy adjustment, you will help yourself, too. God's blessings to you and yours!

—*Michaelene Mundy*

Why Do People Move?

You may not understand why you are moving to a new house. Talk to your parents and other grown-ups to help know why this is happening.

Mom or Dad may have a new job, and by moving closer, they can spend more time with you. Maybe your house is too small for your family. Or maybe it is important now to live closer to grandparents.

Sometimes, moving doesn't take you closer, but farther away, from people you love. But they can visit you and you can visit them. You can even have a fun sleep-over at their house. This might be something you never did before when you lived close by.

So Many Feelings!

You will have lots of feelings about you and your family moving to a new place. You may feel angry, excited, scared, happy, shy, and lonely, all at the same time!

Your parents have lots of different feelings, too. But they know you will discover new things to see and do. There will be new people to meet and places to go. Your family can have many new adventures together as you get to know your new neighborhood.

Moving makes people happy *and* sad. And that's OK. Just remember, you can find happy times in moving, while finding ways to make the sad part less painful.

Saying Good-bye

Before you leave your old neighborhood, take a walk around with your parents. In your mind and out loud, say good-bye to special places, people, and familiar things. You can say good-bye to trees, plants, buildings, and even the neighbors' pets.

Some people have yard sales before they move. This helps get rid of old things they don't want to take with them. You might have some toys and books you don't really want any more and can put them out to sell, too.

It will be hard to say good-bye to some things, and easier to say good-bye to other things, of course.

How You Can Help

You can help pack the things in your room. Mom and Dad will have lots of boxes to put things in—they can give you some boxes and paper to use. Maybe all your stuffed animals can go in a box and you can mark on the outside of the box what is in it.

When you get to your new house, you'll see the boxes that go in your room and unpack them. Your furniture will be there and you can ask your parents to help arrange things.

You felt safe in your old room and you'll miss it. But you and your parents can set up your *new* room to feel safe and cozy. The arrangement may be different, but you can help make it feel right.

So Many Changes!

It will feel strange at first waking up in your own bed, surrounded by your same furniture and toys. When you first wake up, you may wonder where you are.

Seeing a door or window or bathroom in a different place might make you feel scared. But then you'll remember where you are. And soon you can think of something special to do that day to make things seem less strange. After a few mornings, you won't wonder where you are—you will know you are home!

Remember, Mom and Dad and your sister or brother or pet will be going through changes, too. It will help them get used to a new place if they see you trying your best to adjust.

Some Surprises

Everyone will be busy and tired from all the packing and unpacking. For a day or two, you may eat lots of sandwiches, because all the pots and pans aren't unpacked yet and everyone is tired from all the work.

You might think some things got lost in the move. But as you unpack, you will rediscover them. You might see things you haven't seen in a long time and you might see things you have never seen before.

After only a few days, the new house will start to feel like home.

Making the Move an Adventure

Make it an adventure as you discover special things in your new house, yard, and neighborhood.

Mom and Dad may be busy unpacking and moving furniture. You can help with some things and then explore your house and yard. Later, your parents and you can take a walk and see the neighborhood.

You'll get to know your new house and its yard first, and then get to know the neighborhood and the people who live there. Soon, you'll get to know your new school and discover lots of kids your age.

Asking for Help

Don't be afraid to ask for help from Mom and Dad as you adjust to new things and new people. Let them know when you feel scared or worried. They probably have the same feelings now—even as grown-ups.

They probably moved when they were kids, too. They will remember what it was like and can share stories of how they found good things about moving.

If you have a pet, it may feel scared and not understand what's going on. But you can make it feel safe and secure that it still has you—just like you have your parents to watch over you.

Make It <u>Your</u> Home!

Ask your parents if you can help pick paint or wallpaper for your new room. Even if the new house or apartment is already decorated, colors can be changed. You can hang pictures of your friends and old neighborhood in your new room.

Sometimes when you feel bored in the new house, you might think you wouldn't feel that way in your old house. But remember, there were times you were bored in the old house, too. Find things to do here to change bored times to fun times.

If your family is building a new house, ask to see it as it is being built. Walk around inside with your mom and dad to see where all the rooms will be. It can be fun imagining what it will be like with the walls and roof finished, and grass in the yard.

Don't Change Everything!

Even though lots of things may be shiny and new at your new house, you'll want to keep some of the "old" things you are used to.

For example, you'll still want to read a good bedtime story, or have Mom or Dad read one to you. You will also want to keep saying your prayers at bedtime or before meals. And if you put your school drawings on the refrigerator before, keep doing that.

Having some things just like they were before makes you feel like you are really home.

Staying in Touch With Friends

Take pictures of your old house, and pictures of your old friends, to keep with you. Remind your parents to get these pictures developed, so you can put them in your new room right away.

Take pictures of your new house and the new places you're seeing. You can send these to friends now too far away to see every day. You'll have lots to write or talk about as you describe the new places you are seeing and the people you are meeting.

Your New School

Visit your new school ahead of time, if you can. The weeks before school starts, most teachers are in their classrooms, getting things ready. Ask your parents to take you and ask the principal to show you where your classroom will be. Maybe your new teacher will even be there to meet.

Introduce yourself to other kids you meet in the neighborhood. They will probably be going to the same school and know other kids your age. As you spend time with new friends, you'll find things that you like to do together.

Saying Hello

Sometimes neighbors will stop by with cookies or a cake to welcome you. They can tell you and your parents about the neighborhood, and the kids that may be close by. They are just as curious about you as you are about them!

You don't have to wait for new neighbors to come over. Ask Mom or Dad to go with you to introduce your family to them. Making new friends can begin with just saying "Hello"—at church, at school, or around the neighborhood.

"Home Is Where the Heart Is"

There is a saying, "Home is where the heart is." This means that what makes your home a real home is the love that is in it.

You may be moving to a new house or apartment, but the things that make your house a "home" will be with you—your mom and dad, brothers and sisters, your pet. They love you and you love them.

That's what matters most in every home.

Michaelene Mundy has written previous Elf-help Books for Kids, including the very popular *Sad Isn't Bad* and *Mad Isn't Bad*. A former elementary teacher, she has worked with learning disabled children and has also been a family and school counselor. She is now a senior counselor at a private high school.

R. W. Alley is the illustrator for the popular Abbey Press adult series of Elf-help books, as well as an illustrator and writer of children's books. He lives in Barrington, Rhode Island, with his wife, daughter, and son.